A Musical Offering

Hymnfest
For The Church Year

Ruth M. Buenting

and

James Buenting

with

Joy Berg

CSS Publishing Company, Lima, Ohio

A MUSICAL OFFERING

ISBN 0-7880-1527-3   PRINTED IN U.S.A.

In memory of my friend
Inge Iwanowsky
for her
encouragement and assistance

"My heart shall bloom forever
For you with praises new
And from your name shall never
Withhold the honor due."
— Paul Gerhardt

Table Of Contents

Preface

A Musical Offering is a companion book for *Gloria! Letters From Hymnwriters*. This book contains a hymnfest according to the Church Year complete with commentary on the Church Year and descants to some hymns. You will also note that you may include a special musical offering such as the one we chose by J. S. Bach.

While I have written the commentary on the hymns, James Buenting has written and critiqued the Church Year. He is presently serving as pastor of Christ Lutheran Church, Kelowna, British Columbia, Canada. Found in his comments are refreshing insights on our journey through the liturgical year.

Here, Joy Berg has both arranged the verses of the hymns as well as provided original descants to them. She is a candidate for her doctoral degree in conducting (University of Iowa). At the present Joy is cantor at the Lutheran Church of the Nativity (ELCA), Ardeen, North Carolina.

This hymnfest was first sung on 9 March 1997 and was received with overwhelming attendance and enthusiasm. It is our hope that you, too, will enjoy singing the praises of our God as much as everyone enjoyed singing them on that day.

Ruth Buenting
Kelowna,
British Columbia,
Canada

Foreword

One of the besetting sins of our time is what Elton Trueblood once called "the sin of contemporaneity." This is the widespread assumption that "if we didn't invent it, it can't be worth very much." It is the result of a severe deprivation — the absence of rootage in a living and life-giving Tradition. When people find themselves isolated in time from a meaningful heritage, both the past and the future become meaningless to them. The sense of worth and identity which a heritage can bestow, and the sense of purpose and mission which are by the sacred duty of handing on that heritage intact and enriched to the next generation, are both lost. Disconnected from past and future, the present loses most of its worth, too.

Sins begin to lose their grip when they are named and understood. But they release their grip on us only when we are drawn beyond them into something so much better that we leave them behind forever.

The Buentings, Ruth as author and James as pastor, share one mission in life: to get contemporary Christians to leave behind the deadening sin of contemporaneity by enticing us back into the neglected riches of our own Tradition. Ruth achieves this through ingenious "letters" from folks like us, saints of the past. In her deft and direct way she places these folks side by side with us in our world, and before we know it we find ourselves side by side with them in theirs. And, lo and behold, down goes a root from our heart to theirs, and tradition lives again for us.

Packaging these "letters" along with the hymns associated with their "authors," and creating a Hymnfest that takes an entire congregation through the Church Year together, is a stroke of genius from a deeply pastoral heart. When a whole congregation can reconnect with its living Tradition and freshen its vision of a vital part of its mission for the future, its life in the present is infused with meaning and purpose. The full corporate character of the Church, alive in past, present, and future, in time and eternity, on earth and in Heaven, asserts itself once again and sends the sin of contemporaneity packing.

We owe much to Ruth and Pastor James Buenting, and to Joy Berg for her lovely descants. What a memorable experience any congregation has in store for itself that celebrates this unique Hymnfest. It could become a new Tradition!

J. Robert Jacobson
First Bishop
Synod of Alberta and the Territories
ELCIC

A Musical Offering
Hymnfest
For The Church Year

Advent

Letter
"O Lord, How Shall I Meet You"
    Hymnwriter: Paul Gerhardt (1607-1676)
    Tune: Johann Crüger (1598-1662)
v. 1 — choir women
vv. 2, 5 — all

Christmas

Letter
"Hark! The Herald Angels Sing"
    Hymnwriter: Charles Wesley (1707-1788)
    Tune: Felix Mendelssohn (1809-1847)
vv. 1, 3 — all

Epiphany

Letter
"O Christ, Our Light, O Radiance True"
    Hymnwriter: Johann Heermann (1585-1647)
    Tune: Nuernberg Gesangbuch (1676)
v. 1 — choir
vv. 2, 5 — all

Lent

Letter
"Print Thine Image, Pure And Holy"
    Hymnwriter: Thomas Kingo (1634-1703)
    Tune: Genevan Psalter, 1551
choir only

Maundy Thursday

Letter

"O Living Bread From Heaven"
   Hymnwriter: Johann Rist (1607-1667)
   Tune: Johann Steurlein (1546-1613)
v. 1 — women
vv. 2-4 — all

Good Friday

Letter

"Jesus, Priceless Treasure"
   Hymnwriter: Johann Franck (1618-1677)
   Tune: Johann Crüger (1598-1662)
vv. 1, 3 — all

Easter

Letter

"He Is Arisen! Glorious Word!"
   Hymnwriter: Birgitte Katerine Boye (1742-1824)
   Tune: Philipp Nicolai (1556-1608)
choir only

Ascension

Letter

"Look, The Sight Is Glorious"
   Hymnwriter: Thomas Kelly (1769-1855)
   Tune: William Owen (1814-1893)
vv. 1, 4 — men only

Offering

Sheep May Safely Graze, Cantata #208
   J. S. Bach (1685-1750)
organ and piano

Pentecost

Letter
"O Day Full Of Grace"
    Hymnwriter: Nikolai Grundtvig (1783-1872)
    Tune: Christoph Weyse (1774-1842)
vv. 1, 4, 5 — all

Trinity

Letter
"Holy, Holy, Holy"
    Hymnwriter: Reginald Heber (1783-1826)
    Tune: John B. Dykes (1823-1876)
v. 1 — all
v. 2 — choir a cappella
v. 4 — all

Reformation

Letter
"A Mighty Fortress Is Our God"
    Hymnwriter: Martin Luther (1483-1546)
    Tune: Martin Luther
vv. 1, 4 — all

Christ The King Sunday

Letter
"Now Thank We All Our God"
    Hymnwriter: Martin Rinckart (1586-1649)
    Tune: Johann Crüger (1598-1662)
all verses

S.D.G.
Solo Deo Gloria
To God Alone The Glory!

Welcome to our hymn sing for the Church Year. We hope you will enjoy the musical offering that has been left behind by the saints of the Church.

Both the people who wrote the text and composed the music have left a legacy of faith which has endured for generations. However, keep in mind that this is just the merest "nibble" of an unending musical feast which has been left to us.

Together, we will journey through the Church Year praising God just as they did. While on the journey, we will find out more about the saints behind these hymns. We hope that your vision of faith, hope, and love will be enriched through the words and music of these saints!

Let us now glorify our God as we journey in song through the Church Year!

* * * *

Advent

The beginning of the Church Year starts with the four-week Season of Advent. We prepare for the coming of Christ at Christmas as well as at the end of time. It is a time of repentance coupled with joy in anticipation to meet the Bridegroom, Christ Himself.

Dear People in Christ, our loving Savior,

As a young man, I went to Wittenberg to study theology, wanting very much to become a Lutheran pastor. I remained there for fourteen long years.

You see, my studies were constantly interrupted because of the Thirty Years' War. After I had completed my education, it was difficult to secure a parish. There were times when I thought I would stay in Wittenberg forever!

By 1657, I was appointed as pastor of St. Nicholas' Church in Berlin. I was there for ten years. However, the intolerant Reformed Grand Duke eventually issued a statement. All Lutheran pastors were required to sign this document saying that they would not preach against doctrinal differences.

More trouble. As I would not sign the document, my position was cancelled. Two years passed. I was assigned to a church in Lueben, a very difficult parish.

During this time, I encountered personal difficulties as well. I lost nearly my whole family. All our children died except for one. And only one year after I had been dismissed from St. Nicholas' Church, my beloved wife, Anna Maria, died. We were married for only thirteen years. I was left to raise our one son alone.

But whatever the conditions, I found peace in writing approximately 130 hymns. Through the years, people have said that they stand out from any others that were ever written in Germany. They say that these hymns shine with linguistic beauty and sheer simplicity.

But for me, my hymns mirror my deep trust in God and the hope of salvation through Christ Jesus. The composers, Johann Crüger and Johann Ebeling, adorned my religious poetry with exquisite melodies.

Perhaps you have heard of my Advent hymn, "O Lord, How Shall I Meet You." In any and all circumstances, the Lord was always there for me. All I had to do was to meet Him in worship and in prayer.

Is that where you meet Him, too?

Paul Gerhardt
(1607-1676)

Hymn: "O Lord, How Shall I Meet You"

*   *   *   *

Christmas, The Nativity Of Our Lord

As we all know, Christmas is the brief but yet overwhelming celebration of the birth of our Savior Jesus Christ. The entire world celebrates Christmas, and non-Christians are as aware of this festival as we are. How important it then becomes for us to remember the earthly birth of Jesus with song as it was announced to the shepherds on that first Christmas Eve.

15

Dear Ones in Christ,

I understand that you will be singing one of my 6,000 hymns! It was rather hard to keep track of all 6,000. No computer screens to pull them up on, you know! Never mind a computer filing system for 6,000 hymns! I think your computers would have come in quite handy for *all* of my hymns, but such computer technology was not around in my time.

During the eighty years which God granted me, I was busy proclaiming His Word in sermons as well as in songs. However, I must admit that telling His story in music, as in the text of a hymn, was God's gift to me. It was a joy rather than a chore to pen one hymn after another. The words came easily to me, just as your "God-given" talent comes easily to you. For each person has been blessed with a special gift.

I traveled a good deal of my life. Graduating from Christ Church College, Oxford, in England, I belonged to a group called the "Oxford Methodists" there. Several years later, I was ordained.

Immediately, I left England as a missionary to Georgia. It wasn't long after that I became involved with Moravians. I traveled back to London to serve as curate, but once more I left. This time I joined my brother, John, as an itinerate preacher.

Finally, I returned to Bristol, where I served several Methodist Societies. Despite all of this, I still considered myself to be a lifelong member of the Anglican church (although some could dispute this!).

No matter where I served our Lord, I always praised God's Holy Name. On this day we call Christmas, God sent Jesus, the Word, as His gift of love to everyone on this earth.

Please join the angel choir on that first Christmas Eve in singing my Christmas hymn "Hark! The Herald Angels Sing." Echo the praise of the angels.

Christ is born!

Charles Wesley
(1707-1788)

Hymn: "Hark! The Herald Angels Sing"

* * * *

Epiphany

The Birth and Baptism of Jesus was remembered in early Christian history with a special day, the 6th of January, before His birth was officially celebrated. During the Epiphany Season we recall the coming of the Wise Men to worship the Infant Jesus. Since the Wise Men were Gentiles, they came to symbolize to all the world that Christ is the universal Savior of humankind. Missionary work is often emphasized during this time of the early New Year as a reminder that we, too, are to be "wise people" in bringing the Good News ... in bringing the Light of Jesus to the world.

My Dear Friends in Christ, our loving Savior,

I was one of five children born to a poor furrier and his wife. As it turned out, I was the only one that survived, although I, too, was very ill. My mother promised God that I would serve Him as a Lutheran pastor if I were allowed to live. Like Hannah, she dedicated me to the Lord. It was an honour to serve Him as a pastor in His Church.

I served in only one place, Koben, Germany. By 1616, the town was reduced to ashes by a devastating fire. The next year my dear wife died, and the year after that the Thirty Years' War began. You might say that from 1616, life grew difficult for me.

Koben was the scene of intense fighting. It was plundered four times. Each time I fled and was robbed of my possessions. Four times I had to start all over again. Once when fleeing, I was shot at several times. In 1631, the pestilence came to Koben. Now we had not only war, but also illness. The only one to turn to was Christ Himself.

I would have given up, given in to despair. But rather than doing this, I groped through the darkness of war and illness looking for light from Heaven. In "O Christ, Our Light, O Radiance True," I prayed for all to come to the knowledge of our Savior. I prayed for God's grace. One of my 400 hymns, it was printed in 1630 in my *Devoti Musica Cordis* under the section, "In the time of the persecution and distress of pious Christians."

17

Perhaps the hymn I am most remembered for is "O God, My Faithful God." My life was somewhat like those of Paul Gerhardt and Martin Rinckart. We spread God's Word in times of utter devastation. Fools for Christ by the world's standards, we were all "losers" having nothing. Or were we?

Johann Heermann
(1585-1647)

Hymn: "O Christ, Our Light, O Radiance True"

*   *   *   *

Lent

The forty-day and six-Sunday span of Lent is well-known to all of us. During this time of remembering the suffering of Christ for our sins, we are drawn closer to the Cross of our Lord than at any other time of the year. Perhaps no other season of the liturgical Church Year has more well-known hymns than this special time of contrition, remembrance, and gratitude.

(The choir will be singing an arrangement of the devotional hymn "Print Thine Image, Pure And Holy," by Johann Sebastian Bach.)

Beloved in Christ,

I am known as the first great hymnwriter of Denmark. However, I would have never guessed that this honor would be bestowed upon me. I had many difficulties with the hymns I wrote. The King of Denmark was "on my case," so to speak.

After I finished my early schooling, I attended the University of Copenhagen, where I completed my theological studies. After being a tutor for a short time, I was ordained a clergyman. As a parish pastor, I served several churches. Finally, I was consecrated a Lutheran bishop as well as becoming a member of Denmark's nobility.

I not only had parishes, but our many, many children! Officially they were my stepchildren. You see, I married two widows with large families. The children were always coming and going. You know what that's like!

After the death of my second wife, I married a young noble-woman. We had a very happy marriage without any children. My third wife insisted on coming with me on all my parish visits.

During the years, I wrote many hymns. Eventually, the King of Denmark asked me to provide the Church with a new hymnal. However, the King did not like my songbook. Consequently, someone else was appointed for the task. But the next hymnal did not please the King either. A committee, as usual, was then asked to provide Denmark with a new hymnbook. At last the King gave his nod of approval. This new hymnal contained 85 of my hymns.

"Print Thine Image, Pure And Holy," which I wrote, was in the first hymnal that I edited. It was originally a long one on the crucifixion of Christ. The hymn as you know it today is only the fifteenth verse. Because the hymn now begins with a different verse, it is known by a new name. "Print Thine Image, Pure And Holy" is a beautiful title, isn't it?

Beautiful enough to have engraved upon our hearts forever.

Thomas Kingo
(1634-1703)

Hymn: "Print Thine Image, Pure And Holy"

*   *   *   *

Maundy Thursday

It was in the "night in which He was betrayed" that our Lord instituted the Sacrament of Holy Communion in the Upper Room. The old Jewish Passover now took on new significance and lasting benefit for Jesus' followers of all times. It has been said that the world's longest continuous dinner began that first Maundy Thursday evening in Jerusalem. It is a Supper which has no ending until the coming of the Kingdom of God in eternity.

We sing the hymn "O Living Bread From Heaven" to the charming melody of a German folk tune.

Dear Members of the Body of Christ,

The Lord entrusted me with both the spiritual as well as the physical health of the inhabitants in Wedel and the surrounding area. Wedel was located near Hamburg, Germany.

For I was a pastor as well as a physician. This was my only church, although I could have had positions elsewhere. However, I decided to remain with my faithful flock, where I spent more than thirty years. I was only 28 when I settled here. To Wedel, I brought my bride, Elisabeth Stapfel.

In addition to being both a clergyman and a physician, I also loved to write hymns. Approximately 680 flowed from my pen on every aspect of theology. I learned to write them on the "impulse of the moment." I was taught this technique at the university in Rinteln by the hymnwriter, Josua Stegmann.

My hymns were sung all over Germany while I was at Wedel. They were sung in both the Lutheran and Roman Catholic churches. However, one Lutheran church did not sing them. Which one? If you guessed "Wedel," you're right! As the old saying goes, a person is never honored in his hometown. However, that did not matter. Everyone else was singing them all over Germany.

"O Living Bread From Heaven" I wrote for Holy Communion, which in my time was celebrated often. The bread I handed out as a pastor was far different from the bread we all ate around the tables in homes. For it was not only *life-giving* but *living*! And we used one cup, the chalice, representing our unity as the communion of saints.

I attended five universities and was crowned *poet laureate* by the Emperor. While these are blessings, I was concerned in matters of the heart, of the Spirit, just like the beloved physician Saint Luke. You might say Saint Luke and I had much in common.

Even though Saint Luke lived 1600 years before me.

Johann Rist
(1607-1667)

Hymn: "O Living Bread From Heaven"

*   *   *   *

20

Good Friday

The most solemn day of the entire Church Year is commemorated on this day we have come to call "Good." Good Friday may have taken its name from the old expression, "God's Friday." It was on this day that the sun hid its face that our salvation was completed. The Cross has unspeakable and awesome meaning for us.

Dear Precious Ones in Christ,

I lived through the Thirty Years' War in Germany like many others. But the war did not affect me nearly as much as some of my contemporaries. This did not mean, however, that my life was lived out in perfect tranquility.

When I was only two, my father died. Oh! How I wished as a boy and as a man to know my father. For who can replace a father's love? Who can replace another person? Each of us is a unique creation made in God's image. There will never be another person like you. Or even like me.

However, my uncle did adopt me, and saw to it that I received a good education at the University of Koenigsberg. Like my father, my uncle was a lawyer. At Koenigsberg, I followed in their footsteps, taking up this profession.

My greatest accomplishment was not related to being a lawyer or even to the positions which I held. I am primarily remembered for my poetry. Even though I wrote secular poems, it is my poetry for the Church that has endured to this very day. The 110 hymns which I wrote far outrank anything else I achieved during my lifetime. "Jesus, Priceless Treasure" is the most well-known.

Each one of us is precious to God. Our treasure is Christ. On the Cross, Jesus cried out for His Father's love, just as I had cried for my earthly father.

No amount of money could ever purchase the treasure of God's love in Christ on Good Friday. Martin Luther summed it up this way:

"At great cost
he has saved and redeemed me
A lost and condemned person.
He has freed me
from sin, death, and the power of the devil —
not with silver or gold
but with his holy and precious blood
and his innocent suffering and death."*

Many people treasure their wealth and affluence. However, the secret of a real treasure is that you cannot buy it. My greatest treasure as a lawyer? Jesus. What is your treasure?

*Johann Franck
(1618-1677)*

Hymn: "Jesus, Priceless Treasure"

Reprinted from The Small Catechism in Contemporary English *by Martin Luther. Copyright © 1960, 1968 Augsburg Publishing House. Used by permission of Augsburg Fortress.

* * * *

Easter Sunday, The Feast Of The Resurrection

Easter Sunday has been called the "Queen of Feasts," the day of the triumphant resurrection of Christ from the dead. The resurrection of Jesus Christ is the cornerstone of the Christian faith. The New Testament assures us "because I live, you shall live also." So great and pivotal for the entire Christian faith is this day that each Sunday in effect becomes a "little Easter."

Dear People in Christ, our Risen Savior,

I understand that the choir will be singing my Easter hymn "He Is Arisen! Glorious Word!" during this festival season of Easter! It is only one stanza in length. This long stanza is to be sung before the Gospel is read from Easter until Ascension Day announcing the Easter message.

I was born in Bentofte, Denmark. In my early twenties, I married Herman Hertz. At the time we were married, Herman was a forester.

22

I led a busy life just like many of you. God blessed our marriage with four children. However, on the side, I learned German, French, and English. I did this to read poetry in its original language and to translate the hymns of the Church.

In 1773, the Society of the Advancement of the Liberal Arts asked for contributions of sacred poetry. I provided the society with twenty hymns. Later, eighteen were chosen for a hymnal prepared by Lutheran Bishop Ludvig Harboe as well as the state secretary, Ove Guldberg.

Life had been going smoothly. But then, as so many of you know, circumstances changed overnight. Suddenly, my husband's job was gone. Like a pink slip. I approached the secretary of state on the matter of finances. He, in turn, mentioned it to Prince Fredrik. As a result, our two sons were educated by the Prince himself.

Our situation grew even worse. My husband died. Prince Fredrik supported my family now. After three years, I remarried a man from the customshouse, Hans Boye.

During this time, I continued my literary interests. A hymnal was being prepared by the Bishop and the Secretary of State. When the *Psalmebog* came out in 1778, it contained 124 of my hymns and 24 of my translations. In addition, I wrote secular poetry as well as drama which was often performed at the royal court.

I outlived my second husband as well. However, God blessed me throughout my life. He was ever with me. No matter what was happening, I always clung to the words of the Easter Message. Do you? *(Pause)*

Please stand as the choir sings my Easter hymn, "He Is Arisen! Glorious Word!"

Birgitte Katerine Boye
(1742-1824)

Hymn: "He Is Arisen! Glorious Word!"

*   *   *   *

Ascension Day

For forty days after His resurrection, Jesus appeared to His disciples to reaffirm their faith in His gift of eternal life. On a Thursday, exactly forty days after Easter, Christ took with Him His disciples to a mountaintop and from there ascended into heaven. Because of the now-finished earthly story of His life, Ascension Day has been called the "coronation day" of Christ as He returned to God in glory.

Dear Ones in Christ,

What a festive day is ours today! For we celebrate the Ascension of Christ in Heaven. Jesus came to earth born in a lowly stall. He began His earthly ministry when He was baptized at the River Jordan. Three years later, the crowd crucified Him. In three days He rose, victorious. Now He has ascended to Heaven in kingly robes, leaving His grave clothes behind.

I wrote over 750 hymns in all. "Look, The Sight Is Glorious" is one of my finest, or so history has said. Ascension Day is very special, very splendid. The Christian Church mentions it every time the Creed is said. Never let anyone tell you otherwise, for Christ is now reigning as King of Kings!

I was born in Ireland, the son of a judge. I had decided to study law also. However, after reading and reflecting, I entered the ministry of the Church of Ireland (Anglican).

However, I soon went independent. This posed a problem for me as I didn't have a place in which to preach other than "just" buildings. And my preaching attracted many.

This problem was solved though when my wife and I put together our wealth. We used a portion of it to build chapels throughout Ireland where I could preach in "a house of God."

I also was known for being a friend of the poor and needy. During the terrible famine of 1845-1849, God used me to feed the hungry. It was just my nature to work *all* the time. For sixty years, I proclaimed the Gospel throughout Ireland. Eagerly, I preached the Good News of saving faith through Jesus our Savior. Do you get the picture?

But more importantly, do you get the picture of that first Ascension Day sight?

(1769-1855)

Hymn: "Look, The Sight Is Glorious"

* * * *

The Feast Of Pentecost

The Day of Pentecost reminds us that the Church is inspired, guided, and blessed by the Holy Spirit. The promise of Christ on Ascension Day that He would not leave His followers "comfortless" all came true ten days later. On the first Pentecost, the Holy Spirit came as tongues of fire upon the disciples, and enabled them to proclaim the Gospel in many languages. As a result, three thousand persons were baptized. Pentecost has, therefore, been called the "birthday of the Christian Church."

Dear People in Christ,

Some have referred to me as the greatest Danish hymnwriter of the nineteenth century. I am very humbled. However, without the Lord's help, my life would not have been woven with the beautiful threads of His protecting love.

As the son of a Lutheran pastor, I clung to the Christian faith. However, in clinging to my faith, I paid a price. For at university I found myself in constant opposition to the Rationalists. The Rationalists put reason above faith in Jesus, our Lord and Savior. After graduating, I tutored for a while and also wrote poetry.

Then, one day, I received a message from my father. He was ill and was in need of an assistant. I went back to Udby in 1810 and preached my trial sermon for ordination. I did not preach what was "politically correct" at the time, for I confronted the Rationalists right in this sermon.

I paid dearly for my words. Because I was true to the Gospel, my ordination was delayed for a whole year! During the next ten years I wasn't given a parish. Furthermore, I wasn't even allowed to confirm my own children!

25

However, that didn't stop me from praising God. Although I did not write "O Day Full Of Grace," I *translated* this ancient folk hymn. The folk hymn had been sung in Scandinavia since 1450. I rewrote "O Day Full Of Grace" to mark the coming of Christianity 1,000 years before to the shores of Denmark. You see, the Christian faith came here in the year 826.

As time went on, I was fully reinstated as a clergyman. God blessed me abundantly for the rest of my life, and in the end, the King of Denmark appointed me a bishop. I was faithful to my Savior just as He was faithful to me. I preached my last sermon *the day* before I died, just days before my eighty-ninth birthday. God's Spirit was forever faithful to me and His Church.

Because of His faithfulness, I never lost the vision of Christ and His Church in the bad times as well as in the good times. Never lose *the* vision. It is a gift from God's Holy Spirit.

Nikolai Grundtvig
(1783-1872)

Hymn: "O Day Full Of Grace"

*   *   *   *

Trinity

The Festival of the Holy Trinity is one week after Pentecost. It reminds us of the fullness of the Godhead: Father, Son, and Holy Spirit. We live in the mystery and faith of the Trinity, and with Saint Paul confess: "O the depth of the riches and wisdom of God! How unsearchable are His judgments and how inscrutable His ways! For who has known the mind of the Lord? Or who has been His counselor? To Him be the glory forever. Amen." (Romans 11:33-36).

Dear Saints in Christ,

I was a minister in the Anglican Church after completing my studies at Oxford in England. I served for many years in my native country as vicar on the family estate.

26

After this post, I was bishop of Calcutta in faraway India. In this capacity, I had the privilege of ordaining the first native Anglican minister.

During my years in England, I saw much vice. On the other hand, in India, there was a vast sea of people who were in need of the Gospel.

I felt it was also my calling to improve the quality of hymns in the Anglican Church. My superiors liked the many metrical psalms that were still being sung. However, I wanted to sing hymns that were grand and glorious. As a result, I decided that a new hymnal was needed.

This hymnal was presented for use in the Church in 1820. However, it did not get the stamp of approval for which I had hoped. Perhaps you have been in a similar situation. I must admit, I was disappointed.

Several hymns which I wrote were in this hymnal. The one Alfred Lord Tennyson thought was the best hymn ever written was one of mine, "Holy, Holy, Holy." My hymnal was the first of its kind in English. For it was organized according to the *Church Year.*

I was always in quest of the sacred, the spiritual. I wrote "Only Thou Art Holy." The tune to "Holy, Holy, Holy" is *Nicaea.* It is named for the Council which met in 325 A.D. This Council formulated the doctrine of the Holy Trinity in the Nicene Creed.

However, there was good news seven years later. My hymnal *was* published! A role model for others which followed, *Hymns Written and Adapted to the Weekly Church Services of the Year* was printed in both London and New York in 1827. It was one of a kind.

Like our God.

Reginald Heber
(1783-1826)

Hymn: "Holy, Holy, Holy"

*   *   *   *

27

Reformation

Lutherans in particular remember the events of the 31st of October, 1517, when Martin Luther nailed his 95 Theses to the door of the Castle Church in Wittenberg. With the ensuing Reformation, the primacy of God's Word was emphasized. Based on Psalm 46, "A Mighty Fortress Is Our God" reminds us of the enduring stability of a rock-like faith, reflected in this sturdy hymn.

My Dear Ones in Christ,

I am writing you this letter to urge you to keep singing God's holy Word. Sing the hymns of the Church in joy and in sorrow. They will give you strength to face whatever occurs in life. Even death itself.

In addition to translating the Bible, I wrote many hymns. I thought we should all sing the Gospel's message. I believe my most famous one is "A Mighty Fortress Is Our God." You might say it was the "Hymn of the Reformation."

As you will remember, I married my Katie, Katherine von Bora, in 1525. Our marriage was blessed with six beautiful children whom we loved dearly.

I faced many trials in my life. However, there was no trial as great as when our daughters, Elisabeth and Magdalena, died. I would have never survived this near all-encompassing grief if I could not have turned to God in prayer as well as in music — the Gospel in hymns.

No one more dear was ever taken from me than our two daughters. Oh, our precious infant, Elisabeth! As for Magdalena, she died in my arms. Magdalena had been such an obedient child. I never had to reprove her in her thirteen years.

When my friends tried to comfort me at the time of Magdalena's death, all I could say was, "I have sent a saint, a living saint to Heaven." Katie took Magdalena's death especially hard. *I* had to console Katie. All we could do was to sing away our despair. Together, Katie and I sang our hearts out to the Lord.

I encourage you to keep in tune with the Gospel, with its message that Christ died for all ... including our precious daughters. For your loved ones, as well as for you and for me.

God *is* a mighty fortress, indeed!

Martin Luther
(1483-1546)

Hymn:"A Mighty Fortress Is Our God"

*   *   *   *

Christ The King Sunday

The final Sunday of the liturgical Year, which began in Advent, reaches its culmination in the affirmation of the lordship of Christ over all creation. On this day we are reminded that "my eyes have seen the glory of the coming of the Lord" and that on the final Judgment Day all eyes will behold Him as "King of kings and Lord of lords." History remains in His hands.

My Beloved People in Christ,

I remember when the raging Thirty Years' War ended. I never ceased to give thanks for blessed peace! While the war raged on, people fled to our city, Eilenberg in Germany, for protection. You see, it was surrounded by a large wall.

Times grew tough. Although the war was far from over, I had, by that time, already seen enough. The war was ugly. Horrible. All I could do was pray. As I look back, things only grew worse.

My wife and I took in many refugee families who came here. I tell you, sometimes I did not know where I was going to put them or what I was going to feed them. But somehow, God gave me His eyes. I just could not turn these families away.

It was during this same time, in 1636, that the table prayer which I wrote for my children came into print. "Now Thank We All Our God" was a prayer for my children to pray before the noonday meal.

You may not think there was anything for which to give thanks. However, we did have food and shelter, although meager. But most importantly, we had Christ who had gone all the way to the Cross for all victims of this horrid war.

Eilenberg became dirty and overcrowded as a result of people seeking refuge here. With the overcrowding came the pestilence. In 1637, two Lutheran pastors died. That same year, the senior church official decided to move out of the utter misery. This left me to minister to the city by myself. *(Pause)* ... and during this time in 1637, my precious wife died.

Others I loved were taken from me, including my parishioners, who succumbed to war and disease. My heart was breaking. There seemed to be no end to the losses in my life.

At times I buried up to seventy people in one day. I would have never survived the loss and wretchedness going on around me if it had not been for my loving Savior.

If you are facing tough times, turn to Christ, who conquered the grave that we might live with Him eternally. He is the King of kings. He will never leave you. Give thanks in your heart for Christ. *(Pause)* Always.

(Pause)

Stand and sing "Now Thank We All Our God," just as I prayed it with my children.

Martin Rinckart
(1586-1649)

Hymn: "Now Thank We All Our God"

*   *   *   *

The following descants, composed by Joy Berg, may be used with selected verses of each of the four corresponding hymns.

Hark! The Herald Angels Sing

Hail   the Prince.   Hail   the   Son   of

right-eous-ness.   Life   He brings.   Ris'n with hea-ling

in   His wings.   Mild   glo - ry   by.   Born that   we   no

more   may   die.   Born.   Born.

Hark,   the   Her   - ald   an - gels   sing.

Glo   -   ry   to   the   New - -   born   King!

O Day Full Of Grace

A Mighty Fortress Is Our God

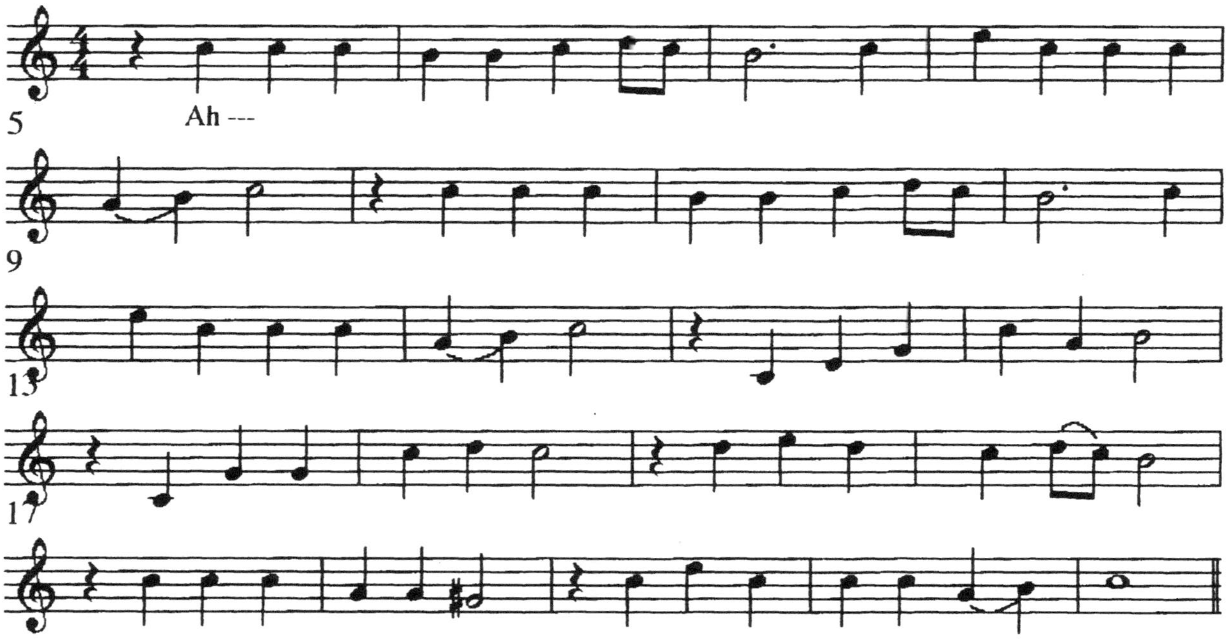

Now Thank We All Our God

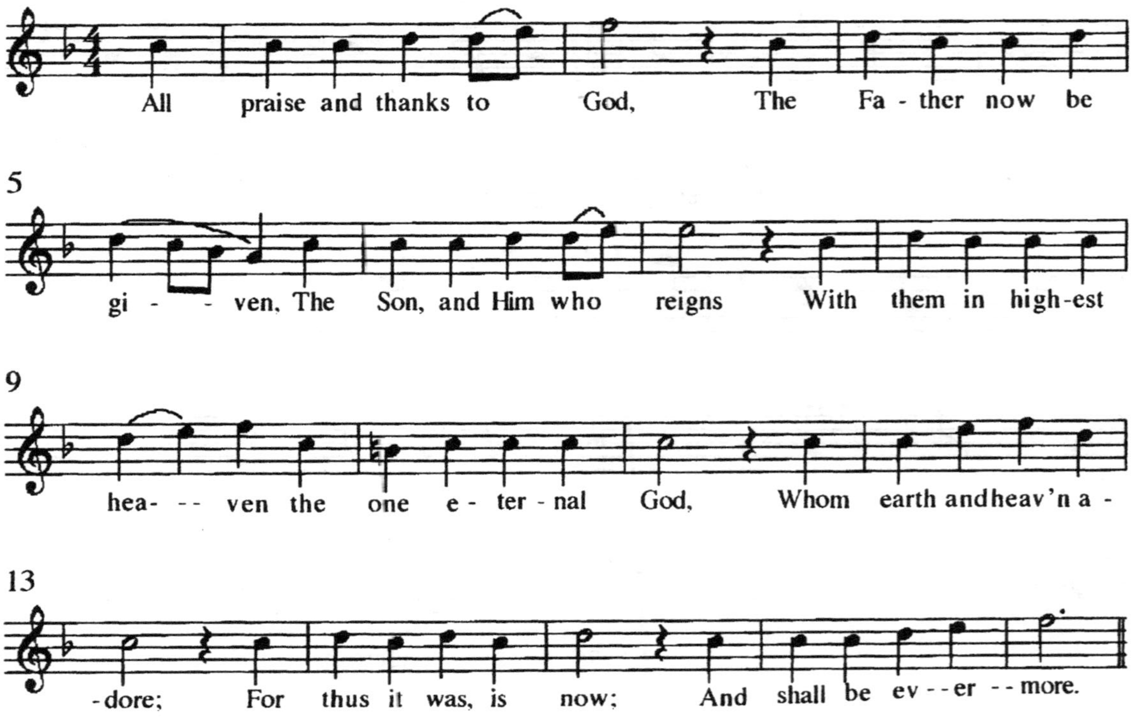

The hyms used in the hymnfest may all be found in the *Lutheran Book of Worship*. Corresponding hymn numbers from the *LBW* for each of the titles used are listed below.

"O Lord, How Shall I Meet You"	#23
"Hark! The Herald Angels Sing"	#60
"O Christ, Our Light, O Radiance True"	#380
"Print Thine Image, Pure And Holy" (*LBW* version of hymn) (J. S. Bach arrangement used by the choir only found in *Service Book and Hymnal* #71)	#102
"O Living Bread From Heaven" (Tune *LBW* #412)	#197
"Jesus, Priceless Treasure"	#457
"He Is Arisen! Glorious Word!"	#138
"Look! The Sight Is Glorious"	#156
"O Day Full Of Grace"	#161
"Holy, Holy, Holy"	#165
"A Mighty Fortress Is Our God"	#229
"Now Thank We All Our God"	#534